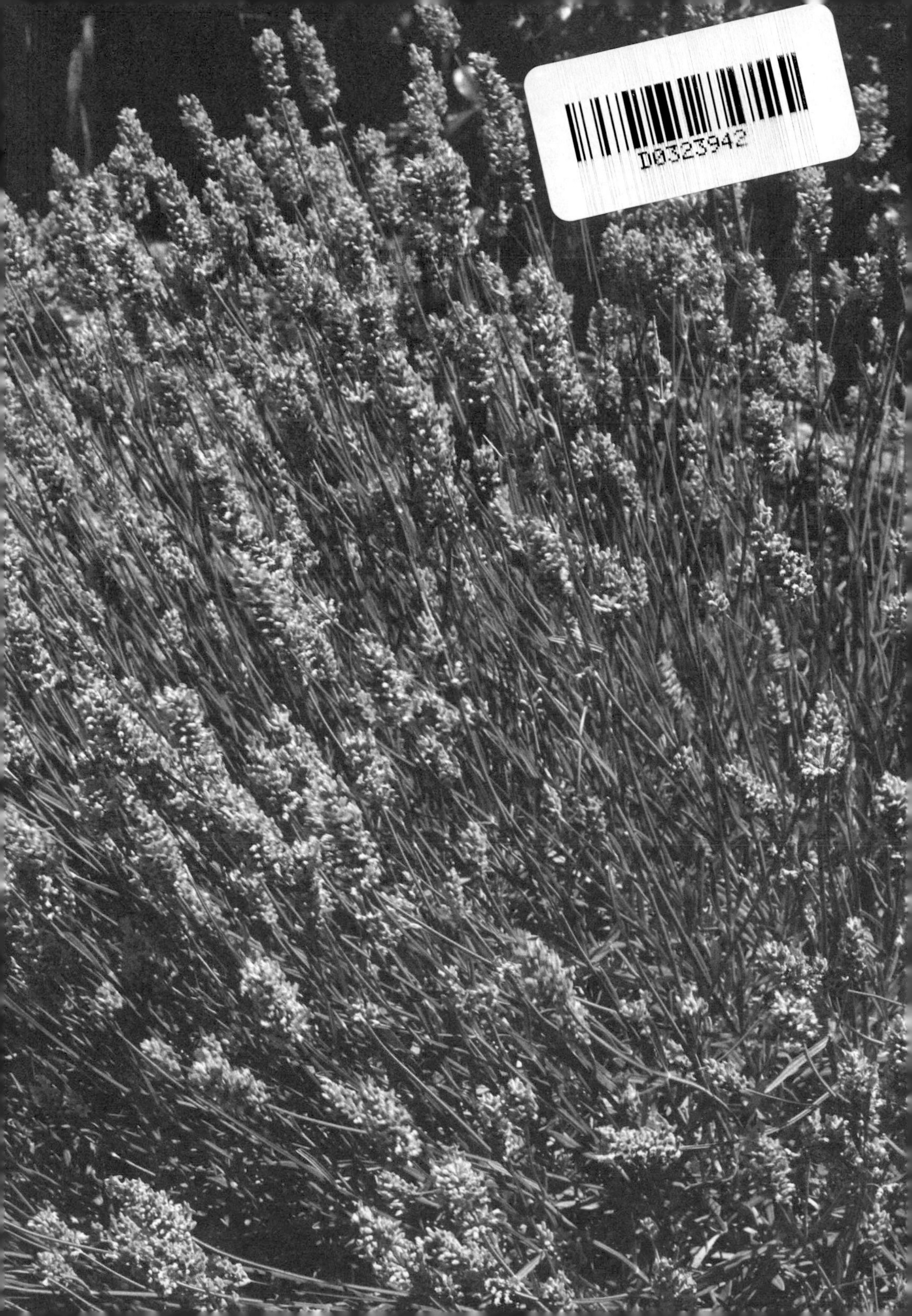

Gardening WITH THE EXPERTS

CAMELLIAS

Gardening WITH THE EXPERTS

CAMELLIAS

J.A.HANSEN

Cover: ***Camellia*** *'Kathryn Funari'.*
Frontispiece: ***Camellia*** *'J.A. Hansen'.*

Published by Harlaxton Publishing Ltd
2 Avenue Road, Grantham, Lincolnshire, NG31 6TA, United Kingdom.
A Member of the Weldon International Group of Companies.

First published in 1992.
Reprinted 1993

Publishing Manager: Robin Burgess
Project Coordinator: Mary Moody
Editor: Christine Mackinnon
Illustrator: Kathie Baxter Smith
Designed & produced for the publisher by Phillip Mathews Publishers
Produced in Singapore by Imago

British Library Cataloguing-in-Publication data.
A catalogue record for this book is available from the British Library.
Title: Gardening with the Experts: Camellias
ISBN:1 85837 030 2

Contents

INTRODUCTION

The genus *Camellia* is a native of the Far East, ranging in habitat over a large area of south-west Asia, China, Japan, Korea, Indo-China, Burma and north-east India.

In China and Japan, the main centres of origin, *camellias* have a long and fascinating history stretching back over many centuries. Originally valued as ornamentals because of the beauty of their flowers and evergreen foliage, the species has many applications. It provides cosmetic, cooking and industrial oils from the seeds; medicines and ingredients for the pharmaceutical industry from roots and leaves; fuel in the form of a high grade charcoal; and above all else, the young terminal growth of *Camellia sinensis*, fermented and dried, is the source of one of the world's most widely used beverages – tea.

The habit of tea drinking was introduced to Europe in the 17th century and was eventually responsible for the arrival of *camellia* plants in the western world. In the 18th century, in an attempt to overcome reliance on China for their tea supply, Europeans endeavoured to obtain plants of *Camellia sinensis* in order to start their own tea industry, but the plants they received from the Chinese, either intentionally or by mistake due to language problems, proved to be *Camellia japonica* and useless as a tea plant. The two varieties of *Camellia japonica*, 'Alba Plena' and 'Variegata', that arrived in 1792, attracted a good deal of attention. They soon became popular as garden shrubs, heralding the arrival of the *camellia* as an ornamental shrub in the western world. Although the popularity of *camellias* has waxed and waned since that time, they are now firmly established in many countries and interest in them has never been greater than it is at present.

Opposite: ***Camellia*** *'Hoylyn Smith'.*

Camellia reticulata.

Laden with flowers, healthy ***camellias*** *in full bloom.*

CAMELLIA TYPES

There are now approximately 200 known species of *camellia*, as yet, not all of them are available outside China. However, for the home gardener they can be grouped under five headings:

1. *Camellia sasanqua*

The name '*sasanqua*' is commonly used to include several other species of similar type and appearance. This is the first of the *camellias* to start flowering each year, usually in early autumn, and they normally bloom profusely until mid-winter, with a few cultivars flowering even later in the year. They have small dark green leaves and small to medium flowers ranging in colour from white through pink to burgundy. They stand full sun, which is required to promote flowering. A number of varieties have a spreading or weeping habit of growth, which makes them ideal plants for espaliering or informal hedges. If

Camellia *'Carters Sunburst'*.

Camellia sasanqua

allowed, other varieties will grow into small trees though they do tolerate heavy pruning.

Some recommended varieties.
Camellia sasanqua:
'Bert Jones' Silver-pink. Medium semi-double.
'Bonanza' Deep red. Large semi-peony form. Spreading growth.
'Chansonette' Deep lavender-pink. Formal double.
'Crimson King' Bright crimson. Single.
'Lucinda' Rose-red. Anemone form.
'Mini-No-Yuki' White. Large peony form.
'Plantation Pink' Pink. Large single.
'Rosette' Rose-pink. Small rose-form double.
'Sparkling Burgundy' Lavender-pink. Medium peony form.
'Star Above Star' White, shading to lavender-pink at edges. Medium semi-double. Flowers later than the others.
'Weeping Maiden' White. Large single.
'Yuletide' Small red single. Slow compact, upright growth.

2. *Camellia japonica*
Japonicas are the best known of all garden *camellias*. There is an infinite variety of form, arrangement, number of petals and size of leaves. The blooms can range in size from miniature (5cm [2in] or less) to large (15cm [6in] or over) and in colour from white through various shades of pink to very dark red. With a number of different varieties, flowers can be seen from early winter through to late spring. The leaves are generally a dark shiny green on the upper surface and a pale green on the underside. Best results are obtained if the bush has some shelter with partial shade.

Some recommended varieties.
Camellia japonica:
'Bon Bon Blush' Miniature. Pink edged white.
'Botan Yuki' (Rusticana) Blush pink with a yellow petaloid centre. Miniature anemone form.
'Desire' Pale pink edged deep pink. Medium formal double.
'Dolly Dyer' Scarlet. Miniature anemone form.
'Ecclefield' White. Large semi-double.
'Elegans Champagne' White with cream centre petaloids.
'Fashionata' Apricot-pink. Large semi-double.
'Grand Slam' Dark red. Large semi-double to anemone form.
'Guest of Honor' Salmon-pink. Large semi-double to loose peony form.
'Guilio Nuccio' Coral-rose-pink. Large semi-double with irregular petals.

Opposite: **Camellia** *'Swan Lake'*.

'Gwenneth Morey' White outer petals with deep cream to pale yellow petaloids. Medium anemone form.
'Kathryn Funari' Deep veined pink. Large formal double.
'Katie' Salmon-rose-pink. Large semi-double.
'Kewpie Doll' Chalky light pink. Miniature anemone form with high petaloid centre.
'Man Size' White. Miniature anemone form.
'Margaret Davis' White edged bright vermilion. Medium sized peony form.
'Mrs D.W. Davis' Blush pink. Large semi-double.
'Nuccio's Gem' White. Medium sized formal double.
'R.L. Wheeler' Rose-pink. Large semi-double to anemone form.
'Snowman' White. Large semi-double.
'Swan Lake' White. Large rose form double to loose peony form.

3. *Camellia reticulata*

The first *Camellia reticulata* to arrive in England was a semi-double form brought from China by Captain Rawes in 1820 and subsequently given the name 'Captain Rawes' in honour of the East Indiaman skipper. Some thirty years later a further *reticulata* arrived in England, sent by Robert Fortune, and was named *Camellia reticulata* 'flore pleno'. Little was heard of this variety for a number of years but it eventually became known as 'Robert Fortune' and has more recently been distributed as 'Pagoda'.

The wild form of *Camellia reticulata* arrived in England in the 1920s, but it was not until the late 1940s and 1950s that a number of different plants that became known as the Yunnan reticulatas from Kunming arrived in the United States of America, Australia and later, New Zealand. This opened the way for extensive hybridising using Yunnan reticulatas and other species, particularly *Camellia japonica*, resulting in a large number of reticulata hybrids with beautiful, very large flowers ranging in colour from pale pink to crimson. The leaves are hard, usually a dull green and with prominent veining. With time, unless pruned to shrub height, *Camellia reticulata's* will become trees.

Some recommended varieties.
Camellia reticulata and hybrids with reticulata parentage:

'Applause' Salmon-pink. Large loose peony form.
'Dr Clifford Parks' Red with orange cast. Large semi-double loose peony form, full peony form or anemone form.
'Glowing Embers' Red. Large semi-double to loose peony form.
'Hoylyn Smith' Soft pink. Large semi-double.
'Jean Pursel' Light purplish pink. Large peony form.
'Lasca Beauty' Soft pink. Large semi-double form.
'Lisa Gael' Rose-pink. Large rose form double.
'Margaret Hilford' Deep red. Large semi-double.
'Moutancha' Bright pink veined white and striped white on inner petals. Large formal double.
'Nuccio's Ruby' Very dark red. Large semi-double with irregular, ruffled petals.
'Pavlova' Clear bright red. Very large semi-double.
'Overture' Bright red. Very large semi-double with upright petals.

Opposite: **Camellia** *'Sparkling Burgundy'*.

'Pharaoh' Old rose. Very large semi-double to peony form.
'Simpatica' Pink. Very large formal double.
'Terrell Weaver' Flame to dark red. Large semi-double to loose peony form.
'Warwick Berg' Clear bright red. Large formal double.
'Woodford Harrison' Deep rose-red veined. Very large semi-double.

4. Species camellias

A number of other species are beginning to become available. This group consists mainly of the small leafed, small flowered, floriferous plants, unchanged from their natural form. They are becoming popular as unusual, attractive garden or container plants but in some cases will not thrive under the same conditions as *japonicas*, *reticulatas* or *sasanquas*. A number of species *camellias* are fragrant, a characteristic which hybridisers are attempting to use to breed fragrance into larger blooms.

5. Camellia hybrids

Hybrids are crosses between two or more species. For example, *camellia saluenensis* hybrids have proved to be more tolerant of soil conditions than other groups; are more cold resistant and sun hardy and they flower well. *Reticulata* hybrids have very large spectacular flowers and, like the *saluenensis* hybrids, are tolerant to soil conditions, but prefer shelter from windy or draughty conditions. They are usually strong growers and need pruning to prevent them growing eventually into large trees. At the other end of the scale, with very small leaves and flowers, are such recent hybrids as *camellia rosaeflora* x *camellia tsaii* and *camellia rosaeflora* x hybrid

Camellia japonica.

'Tiny Princess'.

Some recommended varieties.
Hybrids other than reticulata parentage:
'Adorable' Bright pink. Medium formal double.
'Alpen Glow' Two shades of pink. Miniature single to semi-double.
'Baby Bear' Light pink to white. Miniature single. Dwarf compact growth.
'Daintiness' Salmon-pink. Large semi-double.
'Donation' Orchid-pink. Large semi-double.
'Elegant Beauty' Deep rose. Large anemone form.
'Fairy Wand' Bright rose-red. Miniature semi-double.
'Galaxie' White striped reddish pink. Medium semi-double.
'Itty Bit' Soft pink. Miniature anemone form. Slow spreading growth.

Opposite: Mature ***camellias*** *require routine feeding to bloom prolifically.*

Camellia hybrids.

'Night Rider' Very dark black-red. Small semi-double.
'Spring Festival' Medium pink fading to light pink in centre. Miniature rose form double.
'Spring Mist' Blush pink. Miniature semi-double.
'Water Lily' Lavender tinted bright pink. Medium formal double.
'Wirlinga Princess' Pale pink fading white at centre with deeper pink under petals. Miniature single to semi-double.

SELECTING CAMELLIAS

The range of available *camellias* is now very wide and varieties vary considerably in growth habit, flower form, size and colour, so it is advisable to take some care to select plants that are suitable. Choose a variety you find really attractive, since a good healthy bush, correctly planted, can last for many years.

Your first consideration is the location you have in mind. This will determine the growth habit of the variety that you purchase. Obviously there is no sense in selecting a plant with a low spreading growth habit if the position you have in mind only has room for a narrow, tall growing variety. On the other hand, if you wish to fill a blank space in your garden with a slow growing sprawling plant, you would not purchase a rapid growing columnar type. *Camellias* bloom from cool winter to spring months, according to variety. The best time for planting is autumn or spring, either in pots or containers, or in a sheltered position, or under

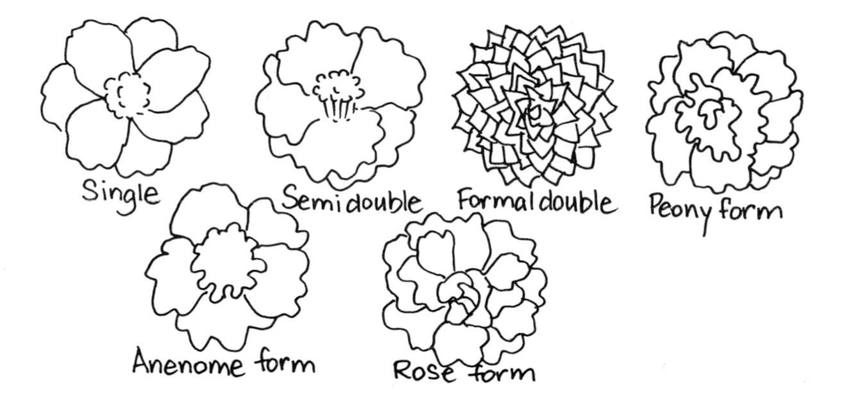

Choose camellias carefully, they can vary considerably in growth habit, flower and size.
Overleaf: Pure white **Camellia** *'Doris Hurst'.*

glass for planting out, according to the variety you select.

A visit to a *camellia* show will provide an opportunity to see a variety of blooms that may help you make your choice. However, it is advisable to do some further checking on the variety you admire. The bloom on the show bench may have had special treatment by way of disbudding, careful pruning, fertilising, or shelter, etc. so that the blooms on the average garden bush may not be quite as big or spectacular.

Perhaps your choice is not free flowering, or can be disappointing as a garden plant. The best way to check on a variety is to see it, if possible, growing in your own region, in a similar situation as planned for your garden. Visit your local nursery to discuss the requirements and type of plant that you are looking for with them.

Finally, having reached a decision, carefully examine the actual plant to make sure it has healthy, glossy leaves, that it is in a pot or bag large enough to suit a big enough root system to support the size of bush on top.

Opposite: ***Camellia*** *'Daintiness'.*

Planting

As already explained, the best time for purchasing and planting *camellias* is during the cool months – say, the last weeks of autumn or early spring. Having decided on a location in your garden, dig the hole approximately twice the size of the root ball. If you have a heavy soil or deep clay subsoil, extra care will be needed with the preparation of the site since it is essential for the plant to have good drainage. Some

Check hole for depth. Container soil should be level with surrounding soil.

Fork the bottom of the hole and mix in compost, manure or peat moss.

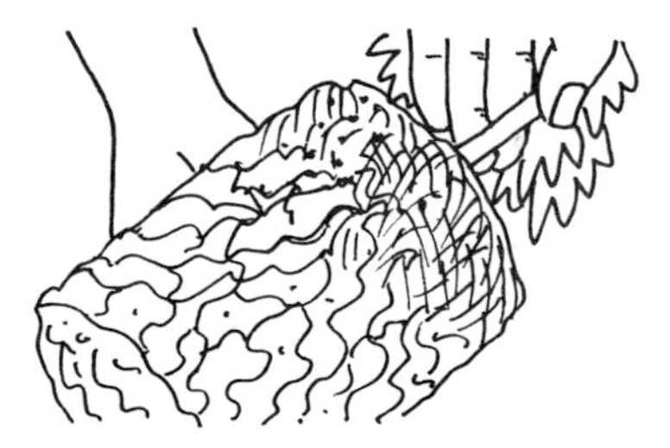

Remove carefully from container. Roots will be easier to remove if the plant has been watered.

Holding plant by stem, place in hole, add half soil, and firm it. Then fill hole, firming the soil by hand.

*Opposite: Choose **camellias** when in flower.*

Camellia *'Moutancha'*.

form of soak-pit or drainage must be provided to carry away excess water. It will be disastrous if the roots stand in water; roots need oxygen and without it the plant can drown. The other extreme is to avoid allowing the roots to become too dry. The problem is to strike a balance between these two extremes: sadly this only comes with experience!

Next, fill the hole with a free-draining soil mixture, containing rotted compost, to supply the humus the plant needs, but which will help retain a moderate amount of moisture, add a small amount of suitable acid fertiliser, ideally a slow-release type.

Before removing a plant from the bag or container, stand it in a bucket of water to give the roots a good soaking, then remove the bag and examine the roots. Ideally there should be a clump of healthy white roots spread throughout the potting mix.

If the roots are embedded in a solid clump with the mix, the plant should be returned and changed for one that has healthier roots!

If this is not an option, free the roots as much as possible and avoid root damage by using a garden hose to spray the roots free of the compacted clump.

The roots must be free to spread into the surrounding ground as the plant matures and becomes established.

Place the plant in the hole and firm the soil mix around it with your fist. Do not stamp on it with your foot as this will put too much pressure on delicate roots and over compact the soil. Make sure the crown of the plant is slightly above ground level, it will eventually settle and it is important that, when finally settled in place, it is no deeper than it was in the bag or container.

Tie the plant to a firm stake to prevent movement in the wind. Some form of shelter overhead, or from a wall or hedge, will also be necessary until the roots are establish in their new position.

A good mulching will initially retain moisture and help keep the roots cool in warm regions, but beware of excessive watering and risk of moisture damage.

By taking some care when selecting and planting your *camellia*, it will reward you by thriving, giving you years of pleasure and needing a minimum of attention.

If you are planting more than one *camellia*, avoid planting them too close together. A distance of 1.5 to 2 metres (5ft to 6ft) apart will prevent overcrowding problems arising in the years to come.

Container Growing

Some varieties of *camellias* make excellent container shrubs, but they do require much more care and attention than those planted in an open garden.

Since the roots are restricted by the size of the container, it is essential to re-pot the plant from time to time. If prudent, it may also be necessary to prune the roots at the same time to prevent the plant becoming root-bound. This will give enough room in the container to add a proportion of fresh potting mix. It is advisable to prune the top of the plant at the same time to compensate for the reduction in roots.

In warm regions or during hot dry weather, the containers can dry out quickly, thus requiring more frequent watering. Some types of containers left in direct sunlight, can become extremely hot in sunny weather and the heat from the sides is transferred to the roots, usually with disastrous results. At the other extreme, in cool regions or where there is a risk of frost, if there is no insulation in the container, for example in plastic bags or pots, again the roots will be damaged.

There is a large variety of containers available, covering a wide range of prices. The choice is a personal one, governed by the price and the purpose for which the container is required. Regardless of choice, it is preferable not to over-pot the plant.

Roots should fill most, but not all of the container, ideally with just 1-2cm (about

Camellia *hybrid 'Itty Bitt' has weeping branches and is suited to container cultivation.*

Camellias *can be grown in conjunction with* **azaleas** *and* **rhododendrons**, *as they have similar soil requirements.*

1in) between the ends of the roots and the sides of the pot, so that the roots are surrounded by a layer of potting mix and do not touch the sides.

As the plant grows the size of the container needs to be increased, or the top growth and roots pruned to keep them within the size of pot required.

Potting mix varies considerably with just about every grower having a personal preference, but the main essentials are that it allows good drainage, is well aerated and is slightly acid with a pH in the range of 5.5 to 6.5.

Assuming your potting mix does allow good drainage, it follows that in hot dry weather your containers must be watered more frequently, particularly if they are situated in a sunny position.

Surround the roots with a layer of potting mix.

As the plant grows, prune the roots.

Partial shade would help in this respect.

There are several advantages with container culture – more plants can be grown in a small area; they are mobile and can be moved around for display purposes on patios, etc; and less hardy varieties may be preserved year round, in accord with the climate of your region.

Give some thought to your choice of varieties, it is a question of personal choice and your purpose for using a container.

There are a number of slow growing *camellia japonica* varieties and small flowered floriferous hybrids or species, that are very well suited to container grown forms of culture.

CARE OF CAMELLIAS

Camellia care really starts at the time of planting. A bush planted correctly and watched over for the first year or two until it is established, will be easier to maintain in good health in the future. Most *camellia* varieties are generally hardy and, once established, will enjoy a considerable amount of sun provided that the roots are kept cool and receive sufficient moisture to compensate for the high transpiration which takes place in hotter climates. Watering is therefore one of the key factors in keeping *camellias* healthy. A good soaking as required, is more beneficial than regular, frequent, light applications that just dampen the surface. The frequent style

Above: ***Camellia*** *'Margaret Davis'.*
Opposite: Camellias make excellent cut flowers that should last several days indoors.

Camellia *'Dolly Davis'*.

Water ***camellias*** *at ground level.*

Mulch the soil around ***camellias****.*

of watering tends to draw spreading roots to the surface where they can be damaged more easily.

Mulching helps to keep the roots cool, conserves moisture where it is needed most and is a source of nutrients. In very hot weather a light sprinkling of water on the foliage in the evening is beneficial, but only after the sun has moved off the plants.

There are many materials suitable for mulching, such as compost, straw, leaf mould, bark, well-rotted animal manures, to name a few.

Water as required before spreading a mulch to a depth of about 8cm. (3in), add a little fertiliser, but avoid stacking the mulch around the base trunk of the plant.

Wrap hessian around the young plant to protect it.

Opposite: Mulch well around plants, to keep the soil cool and moist.

FEEDING

The amount of feed required by *camellias* varies according to the condition and quality of the soil in which they are planted. The best tendency is to underfeed rather than over-feed, so if your soil is of good quality do not be too generous with the amount of feed you give.

Apart from water and air, plants have three main requirements: nitrogen (N), phosphorus (P) and potash (potassium)(K). Nitrogen stimulates stem and leaf growth and a deficiency in this element is shown by poor growth and pale green leaves.

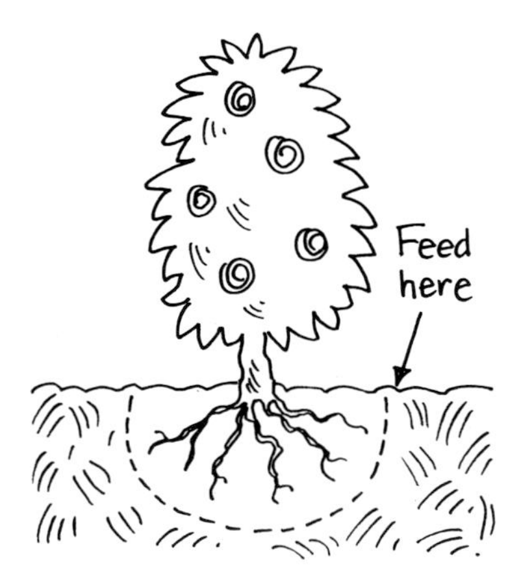

Drip line of the ***camellia****.*

Phosphorus encourages root growth and maturity of flowers, a deficiency is shown by poor growth, bronzing of leaves and inferior flowers. Potash (potassium) encourages firmness in vegetative growth and balances the stimulus of nitrogen. It also improves the quality of the colour in the blooms. A deficiency in potash is shown by some growth restriction and is usually accompanied by a brown margin to the edges of the leaves.

In addition, plants need the trace elements of iron, magnesium, manganese, molybdenum, boron, copper and zinc, which are usually present in the soil in very minute quantities. Consequently the plants only require minute quantities.

There are many suitable fertilisers available from your nursery and appropriate mixes are made up for *camellias*. In general, a balanced food is best, but it can be varied a little each season: in spring a higher proportion of nitrogen; in summer a little less nitrogen and a little more phosphorus; in autumn more potash but little nitrogen.

Whatever fertiliser is used, do not exceed the amounts recommended, if anything, use less than the amount laid down, as it is always preferable to give a little less than too much.

One of the finest foods for plants is well-matured animal manure which contains the three main plant foods including most of the trace elements, in approximately the correct proportions.

An addition to solid fertilisers is foliar feeding, but it is well to remember, a *camellia* can only absorb a certain amount of fertiliser, regardless of the method used and too much at one time can be detrimental to the plant.

Feeding can start in late winter and if using a long term proprietary fertiliser, this will last through until autumn. If using a dry fertiliser, start in late winter with a light application and continue with light applications every two months until autumn. Do not forget, water well both before and after applying the fertiliser. An occasional application of foliar feed on the odd months when not using dry fertiliser can be helpful.

A final word on fertilising.

Newly planted *camellias* do not require feeding for some months. Therefore ailing plants should not be fertilised until after the cause has been established, the trouble has been corrected, or the plant has started to grow and improve in health.

Spoon fertiliser around the plant base.

DISBUDDING

A number of *camellia* varieties are able to set large clusters of buds and as a result the flowers are often small and misshapen.

However, the flowers can be improved both in size and appearance by removing some of the buds; your purpose for the blooms will determine how many buds need to be removed.

If you want blooms to provide a display in the garden, leave two or more buds to each terminal, also leave the buds on the stems. If you wish to use the blooms for show purposes, you will want large perfect blooms, so you must leave only one bud to each terminal.

The buds can be removed quite easily by twisting them off with the fingers, taking care not to break off any leaf or growth buds in the process. Leaving buds of various sizes on the bush tends to lengthen the flowering season. Also the way the bud is facing can affect the quality of the bloom. A downward facing bud has more protection from the weather.

Where large clusters of buds occur blooms will be small and misshapen.

For large, perfect blooms remove all but one bud. Two or more can be left if blooms are not for show.

PESTS

In general, *camellias* are not troubled by many pests and are fairly free of diseases. A healthy, well-grown, well-pruned, open bush will be at less risk than a neglected plant. Regular inspection and frequent hosing down with a fine spray under the leaves as well as on top can discourage pests. Also, good hygiene in the garden, including removing old or dead branches and fallen foliage, can help to prevent pests gathering. Quite often pests can be removed by hand and it is not advisable to spray more than necessary. If you must resorted to spraying do not forget the undersides of leaves, as this is where most sucking insects gather.

Broadly speaking, pests can be divided into chewing insects and sucking insects.

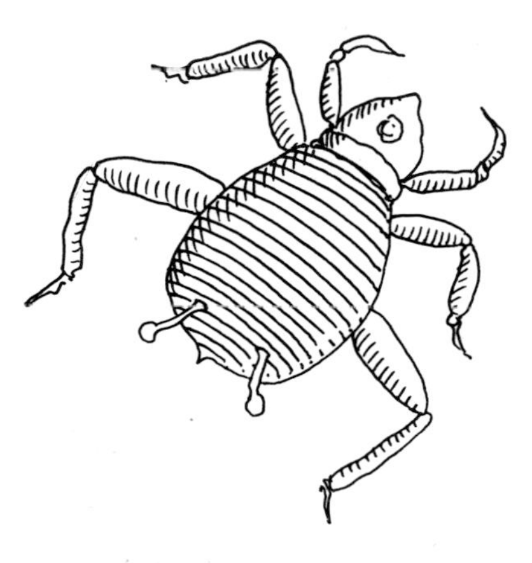

Aphids are attracted to new growth.

SUCKING INSECTS

Aphids: These are sucking insects that multiply very rapidly on young foliage making leaves sticky, encouraging sooty moulds, distorting and twisting leaves. Colonies are exposed and easily killed by spraying with malathion or nicotine. This treatment also applies to the other sucking insects: mites, thrip and scale.

Mites: These insects are difficult to detect as they are invisible to the naked eye and are usually found on the underside of the leaves as a fine red dust. The affected leaves become dull and in some cases defoliation occurs.

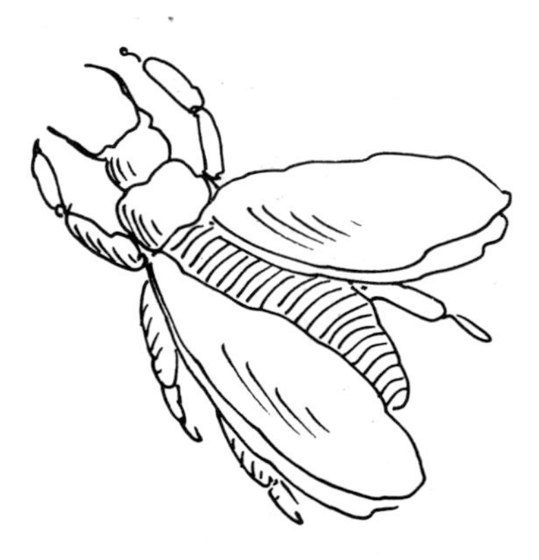

Thrips feed on foliage and new shoots.

Thrip: When infested by this pest, the leaves have a silvery appearance and a brown sticky deposit will appear on the under-side of the leaf.

Scale: The presence of scale is usually indicated by the appearance of a sooty mould on the top surface of the leaves. The scales themselves are on the underside of the leaves and appear as tiny whitish spots or domes.

CHEWING INSECTS

Grass grub: This is a small white soft grub with a dark brown head found curled up into a C-shape in the soil. The adult stage is a small brown beetle which appears at night. An application of diazinon to the ground from late summer to mid-winter will assist in suppressing the grub and a good spraying with the garden hose at dusk can go a long way to prevent the damage to leaves done by the beetle. This is a chewing pest that in high concentrations can strip the leaves.

Caterpillars: Two types of caterpillar are mainly responsible for the damage to leaves: the leaf-roller and the looper.

The **leaf-roller** is found in new leaves which it curls around itself and is therefore difficult to reach with spray. The most effective cure is to squash the curled leaf between the thumb and forefinger! Any attempt to unroll the leaf first usually results in the escape of the caterpillar.

Looper caterpillars are well camouflaged, however they can be effectively removed by spraying.

Spraying with derris or malathion can assist but, as mentioned before, it is difficult to reach them by spraying.

The **looper** is so named because its method of propulsion is to 'loop' along the stem. When it senses danger it rears up and stands motionless like a small brown stick. Spraying is usually quite effective with this caterpillar.

Opposite: The leaf-roller caterpillar is difficult to spray as it wraps itself inside the leaf. Manual removal is the best solution.

Camellia sasanqua *in a sheltered, semi-shaded position.*

DISEASES

Phytophthora cinnamomi: Once again it should be stressed that *camellias* grown in well-drained aerated soil should be relatively free of any disease. However, grown in wet and badly drained conditions or left overlong in polythene bags and containers with poor drainage, the roots are liable to attack by a fungus *Phytophthora cinnamomi*, commonly known as root rot.

It can be treated by bare rooting the plant and soaking the roots in a solution of *captan* provided the plant is not too badly affected. However, the best course is to avoid the condition in the first place by improving the soil drainage.

Leaf scurf: Also called scab or oedema, this is a physiological disorder. It is thought to be caused by adverse water conditions or high humidity. It is believed to be non-infectious.

Dieback: This condition is caused by a fungus infection, *Glomerella cingulata*,. It results in the collapse of an apparently healthy twig or branch. The disease attacks the tissue of the stem forming a canker at the base of the affected branch, cutting off the supply of moisture to the shoot causing it to die back.

Cut the affected branch back to healthy wood and treat the cut with a sealing paint. The fungus can be treated with *captan* or *benlate*. An excess of nitrogen fertiliser will increase plant susceptibility to dieback.

Bud drop: Bud drop can usually be traced to climatic conditions such as a warm spell just before the normal flowering time. However, it can also be caused by a number of other factors such as frost, root rot, bud mites and may occur for a number of reasons: lack of one or more of the essential trace elements in the soil, lack of nitrogen, poor drainage resulting in soggy soil, or soil too dry, root rot and other

Plants grown in sheltered conditions in good soil will withstand disease much better than those exposed to wind or excess sun. Here a trellis offers protection.

Overleaf: High humidity can result in non-infectious leaf scurf.

fungus diseases, and in some varieties exposure of the new growth to too much sun. First check the roots to see if drainage is the problem. If this appears to be satisfactory, check the pH of the soil, which should be between 5.5 and 6.5. It may be necessary to seek the services of a qualified person to do this for you. Where the test proves the soil to be too acid (pH lower than 5.5), it can be corrected with a light application of lime. If the test proves the soil too alkaline (pH above 6.5) it can be corrected by sulphur or sulphate of aluminium. Where the problem is too much sun, the plant should be moved to a more shady position or given some protection, such as shade cloth.

Virus: Virus appears to have little harmful effect on the plant but causes irregular yellow markings or variegation of the leaves or white mottling in the flowers, or both.

Fortunately the virus seems to be transmitted only by grafting or budding using either infected buds, scions or rootstock.

Although virus does not appear to harm the plants unduly, yellow leaves may be prone to sunburn and if yellowing is extensive the plants appear to be less robust than plants of the same variety with solid green foliage.

PRECAUTIONS WITH SPRAYS

All spray materials should be treated with the utmost respect, as a number of them are highly toxic:

- Wear protective clothing, mask, glasses and gloves.
- Read directions on the labels carefully, do not exceed the stated quantity.
- Do not spray on windy days.
- Do not smoke while spraying.
- Avoid spraying in the hot sun.
- Keep all materials in their original containers with lids firmly closed when not in actual use.
- Dispose of empty containers either by burning them or placing them in a refuse bin as soon as you have finished.
- Always keep stores in a locked cupboard.
- Always clean all equipment thoroughly after use.
- Wash yourself immediately after spraying and before eating or drinking.

INDEX